The Politically Incorrect Joke Book

CW00829263

Jimmy Riddle

Billy noticed the goldfish had diarrhoea again

Preface

Dirty Jokes, Political Jokes, racial stereotype jokes even sick jokes. We love them don't we!

This book is a collection of jokes covering sex, violence, puberty and all those taboo subjects that we aren't supposed to find funny.

Political correctness has gone mad. Comedians are attacked with venom for finding fun in some subjects and it's just not right.

All humour has a victim, without a victim there is no laugh. In the UK sick jokes about horrible events are the way that we handle shock and grief – it's just the way we are.

This book is a collection of some of the finest sickest and dirtiest jokes around so sit back and get ready for a good laugh!) Even if you have to hide the pages from those around you)

Thanks for everyone who helped contribute to this collection of the funnier things in life. Thanks also to your sense of humour – twisted though it may be sometimes!

Many of the jokes are original and many have been around for decades we do not purposely steal jokes from anyone, these jokes have no known writer and many are anonymous. For those silent writers we say thank you!

Please be aware that this book contains a lot of material of an adult nature and some of the jokes may cause offence – it's not purposely put together that way and if it does cause offence to some we would like you to know that we couldn't care less ;-) – don't read it if easily offended!!

If you laugh out loud at this book please consider leaving a positive review on amazon for me. There are lots of fuckers out there that don't want to laugh at themselves!

The Jokes

A man went over to his girl's place for a little bit of nookie between the sheets. He presented her with three choices of condom -- gold, silver, or bronze.

"Silver," she said.

"Why not gold?"

"Because I want you to come second for once!"

****
I hear that McDonald's has branches in Africa now.

The customers must prefer them to tables and chairs.

****

I went to the opticians for an eye test recently, & he suggested that I should stop masturbating!

I said that I thought that this was an old wives tale & that masturbating didn't affect eyesight!

He agreed but told me that it was upsetting the other patients in the waiting room!

****

For a couple of months now, I've been getting to know a very friendly young lady who insists on calling me every evening for a chat.

Earlier today, I plucked up the courage to ask her if I could masturbate to the sound of her sexy voice.

I think that's the last I've heard of Anglian Windows.

****

I bumped into my ex in town earlier, I said:

"How's your new bloke?"

"He's twice the man you are," she sneered, "what about your new woman?"

I said, "Thankfully she's half the woman you are, you fat cunt."

****

What's the difference between a Jew and a Pizza?

Pizza does not scream when you put it in an oven

****

I just explained Google images to my mum.

"Pick anything to search for" I told her.
"What about a nice cream pie?" She asked.

"Except that." I replied.

****

I found a video on my wife's phone of me shagging her.

I don't remember filming this but it must have been on holiday, I've got a great tan and my cock looks massive.

****

Genies are tricky little fuckers and will always try to twist what you wish for.

For example, last night I wished that my flat-chested wife could have tits like Angelina Jolie.

****

"I've been waiting for you," she whispered as she bent over pulling up her nighty. "Now get over here and stick it in my arse."

I hate suppository time at Grandma's house.

****

A groom passes down the aisle of the church to take his place by the altar and the best man notices that the groom has the biggest, brightest smile on his face.

The best man says, "Hey man, I know you are happy to be getting married, but what's up - you look so excited."

The groom replies, "I just had the best blow job I have ever had in my entire life and I am marrying the wonderful woman who gave it to me."

The bride comes walking down the aisle and she, too, has the biggest, brightest smile on her face.

The maid of honour notices this and says, "Hey, girlfriend, I know you are happy to be getting married, but what's up, you look so excited."

The bride replies

"I have just given the last blow job of my entire life."

****

A guy walks into an ice cream parlour and asks the owner for a fish and chip flavoured ice cream.

The owner rubs his chin and says "that's a bit tricky, come back in ten minutes."

Ten minutes later the guy comes back and asks for his cone, he licks it and says "Mmmm that tastes great, just like fish. But what about the chips?"

The owner looks pleased and replies "Turn it around"

The guy does this and it tastes just like chips. "Amazing" he says. "Now can I have one that tastes like faggots and peas?"

"That's difficult" says the ice cream man "give me ten minutes"

Ten minutes later the guy comes back and picks up his ice cream. "Mmmm just like mushy peas, but what about the faggots?"

"Just turn it around" says the ice cream salesman with a smile

"Oh yeah, it's just like faggots. Now give me one that tastes like a woman's pussy". Says the guy

"That's difficult" says the owner "give me half an hour."

So the man wanders off, returning thirty minutes later for his ice cream,
He licks it and says "Urghhh! Horrible! That tastes like shit!"

But the owner simply winks at him and says "turn it around".

****
After her fifth child, Lucy decided that she should have some cosmetic surgery "down below" to restore herself to her former youthful glory because her gammon was dangling a bit low and looked like a ripped out fireplace.

Time and Childbirth had taken its toll and she reckoned that, with five children now being the limit, she'd tidy things with a nip here and a tuck there so it looked more like a piggy bank slot rather than a badly packed kebab.

Following the operation she awoke from her anaesthetic to find three roses at the end of the bed.

"Who are these from?" she asked the nurse. "They're very nice but I'm a bit confused as to why I've received them".

"Well" said the nurse, "The first is from the surgeon - the operation went so well and you were such a model patient that he wanted to say thanks".

"Ah, that's really nice" said Lucy.

"The second is from your husband - he's delighted the operation was such a success that he can't wait to get you home. Apparently it'll be the first time he's touched the sides for years and he's very excited!"

"Brilliant!" said Lucy "and the third?"

"That's from Eric in the burns unit" said the nurse "he just wanted to say thanks for his new ears."

****

A girl asks her boyfriend to come over Friday night and have dinner with her parents. Since this is such a big event, the girl announces to her boyfriend that after dinner, she would like to go out and make love for the first time.

Well, the boy is ecstatic, but he has never had sex before, so he takes a trip to the pharmacist to get some condoms. The pharmacist helps the boy for about an hour.

He tells the boy everything there is to know about condoms and sex. At the register, the pharmacist asks the boy how many condoms he'd like to buy, a 3-pack, 10-pack, or family pack.

The boy insists on the family pack because he thinks he will be rather busy, it being his first time and all. That night, the boy shows up at the girl's parent's house and meets his girlfriend at the door. "Oh, I'm so excited for you to meet my parents, come on in!" The boy goes inside and is taken to the dinner table where the girl's parents are seated.

The boy quickly offers to say grace and bows his head. A minute passes, and the boy is still deep in prayer, with his head down. 10 minutes pass, and still no movement from the boy.

Finally, after 20 minutes with his head down, the girlfriend leans over and whispers to the boyfriend, "I had no idea you were this religious." The boy turns, and whispers back, "I had no idea your father was a pharmacist."

****

A man decides to have a party and invites lot of people, telling them to bring their friends. On the invitation he puts "Theme Party -Come as a Human Emotion".

On the night of the party, the first guest arrives and he opens the door to see a guy covered in green paint with the letters N and V painted on his chest. He says to this guy, "Wow, great outfit, what emotion have you come as?" and the guy says, "I'm green with envy".

The host replies, "Brilliant, come on in and have a drink".

A few minutes later the next guest arrives and the host opens the door to see a woman covered in a pink body stocking with a feather boa wrapped round her most intimate parts.

He says to this woman "Wow, great outfit, what emotion have you come as?"

And she replies, "I'm tickled pink".

The host says, "I love it, come on in and join the party".

A couple of minutes later the doorbell goes for the third time, and the host opens the door to see two blokes from Jamaica, stark naked, one with his penis stuck in a bowl of custard and the other with his penis stuck in a pear.

The host is really shocked and says, "What the hell are you doing? You could get arrested for standing like that out here in the street. What emotion is this supposed to be?"

The Jamaican replies, "Well, I'm fucking dis-custard and my friend here has come in dis-pear."

****

The difference between sexes!!!

How to Shower Like a Woman

1. Take off clothing and place it in sectioned laundry hamper according to lights and darks.

2. Walk to bathroom wearing long dressing gown. If you see husband along the way, cover up any exposed areas.

3. Look at your womanly physique in the mirror - make mental note to do more sit-ups.

4. Get in the shower. Use face cloth, arm cloth, leg cloth, long loofah, wide loofah, and pumice stone.

5. Wash your hair once with cucumber and sage shampoo with 43 added vitamins.

6. Wash your hair again to make sure it's clean.

7. Condition your hair with grapefruit mint conditioner enhanced with natural avocado oil. Leave on hair for 15 minutes.

8. Wash your face with crushed apricot facial scrub for 10 minutes until red.

9. Wash entire rest of body with ginger nut and Jaffa cake body wash.

10. Rinse conditioner off hair.

11. Shave armpits and legs.

12. Turn off shower.

13. Squeegee off all wet surfaces in shower. Spray mould spots with Tilex.

14. Get out of shower. Dry with towel the size of a small country. Wrap hair in super absorbent towel.

15. Check entire body for zits, tweeze hairs.

16. Return to bedroom wearing long dressing gown and towel on head.

17. If you see husband along the way, cover up any exposed areas.

How to Shower Like a Man

1. Take off clothes while sitting on the edge of the bed and leave them in a pile.

2. Walk naked to the bathroom. If you see wife along the way, shake nob at her making the 'woo-woo' sound.

3. Look at your manly physique in the mirror. Admire the size of your nob and scratch your ass.

4. Get in the shower.

5. Wash your face

6. Wash your armpits.

7. Blow your nose in your hands and let the water rinse them off.

8. Make fart noises (real or artificial) and laugh at how loud they sound in the shower.

9. Spend majority of time washing privates and surrounding area.

10. Wash your butt, leaving those coarse butt hairs stuck on the soap.

11. Shampoo your hair.

12. Make a Shampoo Mohawk.

13. Pee.

14. Rinse off and get out of shower.

15. Partially dry off. Fail to notice water on floor because curtain was hanging out of tub the whole time.

16. Admire nob size in mirror again.

17. Leave shower curtain open, wet mat on floor, light and fan on.

18. Return to bedroom with towel around your waist. If you pass wife, pull off towel, shake nob at her and make the 'woo-woo' sound again.

19. Throw wet towel on bed.

****

Back in the Swinging Sixties, Michael Caine is holding a big Showbiz party in his swanky new house.

Everyone who's anyone is there - top stars from the worlds of movies and music, fashion and art.

There's a feast of pints, the best wines that money can buy, oysters, champagne,

Lennon and McCartney are helping themselves at the bar, Jim Morrison and his band are sitting on the couch singing "Light My Fire", and over in the corner, George Peppard's getting very friendly with Sophia Loren.

All's going really well, until Jim Morrison decides he's bored out of his skull, and wants to go home for an early night curled up with a good book.

"Oi, Jim," objects Michael Caine, "party's just got started. How's about I get one of 'the ladies' to take you into the spare bedroom for a bit of the 'how's your father?'"

"Fair play," nods Jim [well that's not his exact words, but you get the gist], "as long as she does the rest of the band, too."
"Not a problem, Jim," smiles Michael, as he pulls a young dolly bird in close and whispers some instructions in her ear.

Half an hour later, the young lass is just wiping her chin, when in walks Ringo Starr from the Beatles. "Alright, luv?" he drones, "don't suppose you fancy extending that service to me, do you?"

The young woman thinks about this for a second, then says "What the hell!" and proceeds to unzip Ringo's fly and get to work.

Ringo's having a grand time, until, mere moments before the end, the door opens and Michael Caine bursts in. He grabs the young one by the back of the hair and Slaps her hard across the face! "Wh-what was that for?" she whimpers.

"I told you," Caine snarls

(You're gonna love this)

(Wait for it)

"You're only supposed to blow the bloody Doors off..."

****

A prisoner escapes from his C-Max prison where he had been kept for 15 years.

As he runs away, he finds a house and breaks into it. He finds a young couple in bed. He gets the guy out of bed, ties him up on a chair, ties up the woman to the bed and while he gets on top of her, he kisses her on the neck, then gets up, and goes to the bathroom.

While he is there, the husband tells his wife: "Listen, this guy is a prisoner, look at his clothes! He probably spent a lot of time in prison, and has not seen a woman in years. I saw the way he kissed your neck. If he wants sex, don't resist, don't complain, just do what he tells you, give him satisfaction. This guy must be dangerous, if he gets angry, he will kill us both. Be strong, honey. I love you"

To which the wife responds, "He was not kissing my neck. He was whispering in my ear... He told me that he found you very sexy, and asked if we kept any Vaseline in the bathroom. Be strong, honey. I love you too..."

****

An old man decides that he wants a pet, and goes to the local pet shop to buy a hamster. He gets it home, plays with it, feeds it, and eventually goes to bed.

The next morning he goes to check on his new little friend and it's dead.

He carefully lifts its lifeless body from the cage and heads for the shop to complain. "This hamster I bought yesterday is dead!"

"I'm sorry sir, but there's nothing I can do. They're such tiny creatures and they don't live all that long anyway".

"But I bought it only yesterday!"

"I'm sorry sir, but it was in perfect health when it left the store. There's nothing I can do, except......."

"Yes?"

"There's one thing you could try. I have a recipe. You can make it into jam - I hear it's quite nice".

"JAM? We are talking about a dead animal!"

"Sir, I am just suggesting a way to put the poor departed animal to use"

So the man takes the hamster and the recipe home. He duly makes the jam, and when he gets up the following morning decides to spread some on his toast and try it.
He takes one bite and is utterly disgusted at the taste. He throws the entire jar out of the window and goes off to work.

That evening he comes home from work to find his garden covered with a thick carpet of daffodils. He puts 2 and 2 together and decides to go back to the pet shop.
"Not only did my hamster die, but now my beautiful lawn is covered with daffodils! And all because of that stupid jam idea!"

"That's very odd sir. You see, normally you get tulips from hamster jam......."

****

What would you do?????

You are driving along in your car on a wild, stormy night.

You pass by a bus stop, and you see 3 people waiting for the bus:

1. An old lady who looks as if she's about to die.
2. An old friend who once saved your life.
3. The perfect partner you have been dreaming about.

Which one would you choose to offer a ride to, knowing that there could only be one passenger in your car?

This is a moral/ethical dilemma that was once actually used as part of a job application.

You could pick up the old lady, because she is going to die, and thus you should save her first; or you could take the old friend because he once saved your life, and this would be the perfect chance to pay him back. However, you may never be able to find your perfect dream lover again.

The candidate who was hired (out of 2000 applicants) had no trouble coming up with an answer:

"I would give the car keys to my old friend and let him take the old lady to the hospital. And I would stay behind and wait for the bus with the woman of my dreams."

However, the correct answer is to run the old lady over and put her out of her misery, shag the perfect partner against the bus stop, and drive off for a beer with the old friend!

****

A guy walks into a bar and sees a man sitting at the end with the smallest head he's ever seen. In fact, it is only about two inches high.

So, he sits down next to him and asks, "How is that you have such a small head?"

The man replies, "Well you see, I was stranded on a deserted island and was combing the beach, when I came across an ornate bottle. When I opened it to see what was inside, a beautiful genie appeared and told me that I would be granted three wishes. My first wish was for a luxurious boat to take me home."

The man continues, "A large yacht appeared just off shore. Then for my second wish, I asked to be wealthy, so I would want for nothing when I got home."

The man goes on, "After a large pile of gold coins appeared on the deck of the yacht, I asked to make passionate love to the genie for my third wish. The genie told me that she could not do that, so I asked, 'How about a little head?'"

****

One day a horse and a chicken were playing in the field.

The horse was giving the chicken a ride round the field the chicken asked the horse to jump over a hedge so the horse jumped over the hedge and got stuck in a bog.

The horse asked the chicken to go and get help the chicken ran to find the farmer but could not find him so the chicken took the farmers BMW Z8 and drove back to the horse.

The chicken though the horse a rope and tied the other end to the car and pulled the horse free the horse thanked the chicken and said he would repay the chicken one day if he needed help.

A couple of days later they were playing in the field again and the horse was running towards the hedge when he remembered about the bog and stopped.

The chicken flow of his back and landed in the bog then the chicken asked the horse to go and get the farmer the horse said it would take too long and stood over the bog above the chicken and asked the chicken to talk dirty to him the chicken asked why the horse replied just do it !

So, the chicken started talking dirty to him the horse got aroused and took a hard on then the horse told the chicken to grip the end of his dick then the horse stepped over the bog saving the chicken.

The moral of the story is ......

You don't need a fancy car to pull the chicks when you're hung like a horse

****

A man was visiting his wife in hospital where she had been in a coma for several years. On this visit he decides to rub her left breast instead of just talking to her. On doing this, she lets out a sigh.

The man runs out and tells the doctor, who says this is a good sign and suggests he should try rubbing her right breast to see if there is any reaction. The man goes in and rubs her right breast and this brings a moan.

From this, the doctor suggests that the man should go in and try oral sex, saying he will wait outside as it is a personal act and he doesn't want the man to be embarrassed.

The man goes in and then comes out about five minutes later, white as a sheet and tells the doctor his wife is dead. The doctor asked what happened.

The man replied, 'She choked.'

****

This guy was taking his son on a road trip...and the man pulls out a bottle of beer. The son looking so amazed goes "Dad can I have one?"

The man replies "Can your dick touch ur arse.

The son says "No" the dad replies "Then you're not old enough" A few miles later the dad pulls out a cigarette. The son says "Dad can I have a drag"

The dad goes "Can your dick touch your arse.

The son replies once more "No"...The dad then stops off at a gas station noticing that his son isn't having too much fun and buys him a ice cream and a lottery ticket...Turns out the lottery ticket was a winning one.. The dad then goes to the son "Hey how bout u share some of that with your old man"

The son then replies "Can your dick touch ur arse

And the dad in excitement bursts out screaming "Yes Yes Yes!" and the son replies....

"Good...go fuck yourself then

****

A 12 year old boy walks into a brothel dragging a piece of string, tied to the end of it is a dead frog.

He approaches the 'Madam' and says, "I want a girl but she must have a sexually transmittable disease!"

The Madam looks horrified and replies that all her girls are clean, and besides they don't cater for little boys!

The boy slaps £200 on the counter.

The Madam tells him to go up to a room and the girl will be with him very soon. He says again that the girl MUST have a sexually transmittable disease.

Half an hour later the boy is leaving the brothel, still dragging the dead frog behind him. The Madam can't contain her curiosity and asks him why on earth would he want a girl with a sexually transmittable disease?

The boy replies, "When I get home I'll screw the babysitter and she will get the disease. Then when my dad takes her home he will screw her and he will catch the disease.

When my dad gets home he will screw my mum and give her the disease, and tomorrow when my dad has gone to work the milkman will call round and shag my mum and he will catch it too.

And he's the bastard that killed my frog!"
****

Into a Belfast pub comes Paddy Murphy, looking like he'd just been run over by a train. His arm is in a sling, his nose is broken, his face is cut and bruised and he's walking with a limp.

"What happened to you?" asks Sean, the bartender.

"Jamie O'Conner and me had a fight," says Paddy.

"That little shit, O'Conner," says Sean, "He couldn't do that to you, he must have had something in his hand."

"That he did," says Paddy, "a shovel is what he had, and a terrible lickin' he gave me with it."

"Well," says Sean, "you should have defended yourself; didn't you have something in your hand?"

"That I did," said Paddy. "Mrs. O'Conner's breast, and a thing of beauty It was, but useless in a fight."

****

An Irishman who had a little too much to drink is driving home from the city one night and, of course, his car is weaving violently all over the road.

A cop pulls him over. "So," says the cop to the driver, "where have ya been?"

"Why, I've been to the pub of course," slurs the drunk.

"Well," says the cop, "it looks like you've had quite a few to drink this evening."

"I did all right," the drunk says with a smile.

"Did you know," says the cop, standing straight and folding his arms across his chest, "that a few intersections back, your wife fell out of your car?"

"Oh, thank heavens," sighs the drunk. "For a minute there, I thought I'd gone deaf."

****

Brenda O'Malley is home making dinner, as usual, when Tim Finnegan arrives at her door.

"Brenda, may I come in?" he asks. "I've somethin'to tell ya."

"Of course you can come in, you're always welcome, Tim. But where's my husband?"

"That's what I'm here to be tellin' ya, Brenda. There was an accident down at the Guinness brewery..."

"Oh, God no!" cries Brenda. "Please don't tell me..."

"I must, Brenda. Your husband Shamus is dead and gone. I'm sorry."

Finally, she looked up at Tim. "How did it happen, Tim?"

"It was terrible, Brenda. He fell into a vat of Guinness Stout and drowned."

"Oh my dear Jesus! But you must tell me true, Tim. Did he at least go quickly?"

"Well, no Brenda... no. Fact is, he got out three times to pee."

****

Mary Clancy goes up to Father O'Grady after his Sunday morning service, and she's in tears.

He says, "So what's bothering you, Mary my dear?"

She says, "Oh, Father, I've got terrible news. My husband passed away last night."

The priest says, "Oh, Mary, that's terrible. Tell me, Mary, did he have any last requests?"

She says, "That he did, Father...

"The priest says, "What did he ask, Mary?

She says, "He said, 'Please Mary, put down that damn gun...'

****

Bless me Father, for I have sinned. I have been with a loose woman."

The priest asks, "Is that you, little Tommy Shaughnessy?"

"Yes, Father, it is."

"And who was the woman you were with?"

I can't be tellin' you, Father. I don't want to ruin her reputation."

"Well, Tommy, I'm sure to find out sooner or later, so you may as well tell me now."

"Was it Brenda O'Malley?"

"I cannot say." "I'll never tell."

"Was it Liz Shannon?"

"I'm sorry, but I'll not name her."

"Was it Cathy Morgan?"

"My lips are sealed."

"Was it Fiona McDonald, then?"

"Please, Father, I cannot tell you."

The priest sighs in frustration. "You're a steadfast lad, Tommy Shaughnessy, and I admire that. But you've sinned, and you must atone. You cannot attend church for three months. Be off with you now."

Tommy walks back to his pew. His friend Sean slides over and whispers, "What'd you get?"

"Three month's vacation and five good leads," says Tommy

****

A drunk staggers into a Catholic Church, enters a confessional booth, sits down but says nothing. The Priest coughs a few times to get his attention but the drunk just sits there.

Finally, the Priest pounds three times on the wall. The drunk mumbles, "ain't no use knockin', there's no paper on this side either".

****

Jack was a successful lawyer but he was increasingly hampered by incredible headaches. When his career and love life started to suffer, he sought medical help.

After being referred from one specialist to another, he finally came across an old country doctor who solved the problem.

"The good news is that I can cure your headaches ... The bad news is that it will require castration. You have a very rare condition, which causes your testicles to press up against the base of your spine, and the pressure creates a terrible headache. The only way to relieve the condition is to remove your testicles."

Jack was shocked and depressed. He wondered whether he had anything to live for. He couldn't even concentrate long enough to answer his own question, so he decided he had no choice but to go under the knife.

When he left the hospital after the surgery he was without a headache for the first time in 20 years, but he also felt like he was missing an important part of himself.

As he walked down the street, he realized that he felt like a different person. He could make a new beginning and live a new life.

He saw a men's clothing store and thought: "That's what I need ... a new suit." He entered the shop and told the salesman, "I'd like a new suit", and picked one out.

The elderly tailor eyed him briefly and said, "Let's see, size 44 long." Jack laughed, "That's right, how did you know?"

"Been in the business 60 years." Jack tried on the suit and it fit him perfectly. As Jack admired himself, the salesman said, "How about a new shirt?"

Jack thought for a moment then said, "Sure." The salesman eyed Jack, and said, "34 sleeve and a 16 1/2 neck." Jack was surprised, "That's right, how did you know?"

"Been in the business 60 years."

Jack tried on the shirt, and it fit perfectly. As Jack adjusted the collar in the mirror, the salesman said, "How about new shoes?"

Jack was on a roll and said, "Sure." The salesman eyed
Jack's feet, and said, "Let's see. 9 1/2 E." Jack was astonished, "How did you know?"

"Been in the business 60 years."

Jack tried on the shoes and they fit perfectly. Jack walked comfortably around the shop and the salesman said, "How about some new underwear?"

Jack thought for a second, and said, "Sure." The salesman stepped back, eyed Jack's waist and said,"Let's see ... size 36."

Jack laughed, "Ah ha. I got you! I've worn size 32 since I was 18 years old.

The salesman shook his head, "You can't wear size 32. A 32 underwear would press your testicles up against your spine and give you a hell of a headache!!

****

Two Mexicans have been lost in the desert for weeks, and they're at death's door.

As they stumble on, hoping for salvation in the form of an oasis or something similar, they suddenly spy, through the heat haze, a tree, off in the distance.

As they get closer, they can see that the tree is draped with rasher upon rasher of bacon. There's smoked bacon, crispy bacon, life-giving juicy nearly- raw bacon, all sorts.

"Hey, Pepe" says the first bloke (Don Pedro). "ees a bacon tree!!! We're saved!!!"

"You're right, amigo!" says Pepe.

So Pepe goes on ahead and runs up to the tree salivating at the prospect of food. But as he gets to within five feet of the tree, there's the sound of machine gun fire, and he is shot down in a hail of bullets.

His friend quickly drops down on the sand, and calls across to the dying Pepe. "Pepe!! Pepe!! Que pasa hombre?"

With his dying breath Pepe calls out.... "Ugh, run, amigo, run!! Ees not a Bacon Tree"

"ees... a.... Ham bush"

****

A farmer goes out to his field one morning only to find all of his cows frozen solid. As far as the eye can see are cows, motionless like statues.

It had been a cold night, but he'd never thought anything like this would happen.

The realisation of the situation then dawned on him. With his entire livestock gone, how would he make ends meet? How would he feed his wife and kids? How would he pay the mortgage?

He sat with his head in his hands, trying to come to terms with his impending poverty.

Just then, an elderly woman walked by, "What's the matter?" asked the old lady. The farmer gestured toward the frozen cows and explained his predicament to the woman.

Without hesitation the old woman smiled and began to rub one of the cows' noses. After a few seconds the cow began to twitch and was soon back to normal and chewing the cud.

One by one the old woman defrosted the cows until the whole field was full of healthy animals.

The farmer was delighted and asked the woman what she wanted as a repayment for her deed. She declined his offer and walked off across the field.

A passer-by who had witnessed the whole thing approached the farmer. "You know who that was don't you?" asked the passer-by.

"No" said the farmer...

"That was Thora Hird." (Corny but it made me giggle)
(if you are not from the UK then you just will not get this ... sorry)

****

A husband is at home watching a football game when his wife interrupts, "honey, could you fix the light in the hallway? It's been flickering for weeks now"

He looks at her and says angrily; "fix the light, now? Does it look like I have an electrician logo printed on my forehead? I don't think so!"

The wife asks, "Well then, could you fix the fridge door? It won't close right" To which he replied, "Fix the fridge door? Does it look like I have Hotpoint written on my forehead? I don't think so!"

"Fine", she says "then you could at least fix the steps to the front door? They're about to break". "I'm not a damn carpenter and I don't want to fix the steps!" he says. "Does it look like I have Woodies DIY written on my forehead? I don't think so!"

"I've had enough of you. I'm going to the bar!!!" So he goes to the bar and drinks for a couple of hours. He starts to feel guilty about how he treated his wife, and decides to go home and help out.

As he walks into the house he notices the steps are already fixed. As he enters the house, he sees the hall light is working. As he goes to get beer, he notices the fridge door is fixed. "Honey", he asks, "how'd all this get fixed?"

She said, "Well, when you left I sat outside and cried. Just then a nice young man asked me what was wrong, and I told him. He offered to do all the repairs, and all I had to do was either go to bed with him or bake a cake"

He said, "So what kind of cake did you bake him?" She replied, "hellooooo....... do you see Delia Smith written on my forehead? I don't think so!"

****

George W. Bush is hanging out with the Queen of England. He asks her:

"Your Majesty, how do you run such an efficient government? Are there any tips you can give to me?"

The Queen says: "Well, the most important thing is to surround yourself with intelligent people."

Bush frowns and replies: "Well, how do I know the people around me are really intelligent?"

The Queen takes a little sip of tea and says: "Oh, that's easy. You just ask them to answer an intelligence riddle."

The Queen pushes the button on her intercom and says: "Please send Tony Blair in here, would you?"

Tony Blair walks into the room and says: "Yes, my Queen?"

The Queen smiles at Tony and says: "Tony, answer me this, please. Your mother and father have a child. It's not your brother and it's not your sister. Who is it?"

Without pausing for a moment, Tony Blair says: "Well, that would be me."!

The Queen smiles and says: "Yes! Very good. Thank you!"

Back at the White House, Bush is a bit puzzled. He asks to speak with Vice President Dick Cheney.

"Hey Dick, answer this for me, would you? Your mother and your father have a child. It's not your brother and it's not your sister. Who is it?"

Dick Cheney frowns and says: "Geez, I'm not sure. Lemme get back to you on that one."

Dick Cheney goes to all his advisors and asks everyone he can but no one can give him an answer. Finally, he ends up in the men's room and recognizes Colin Powell's shoes in the next stall.

Dick shouts over to him: "Hey Colin! Can you answer this for me? Your mother and father have a child and it's not your brother or your sister. Who is it?"

Colin Powell flushes and yells back: "Hey, that's easy. It's me!"

Dick Cheney smiles and yells: "Thanks!"

Cheney goes back to the Oval Office and tells Bush: "Hey, I finally figured out the answer to that riddle! It's Colin Powell!"

Bush gets up and angrily stomps over to Dick Cheney and yells right into Dick's face: "No you idiot! It's Tony Blair!"

****

Two bored casino dealers are waiting at the crap table. A very attractive blonde woman arrived and bet twenty thousand dollars on a single roll of the dice.

She said, "I hope you don't mind, but I feel much luckier when I'm completely nude."

With that, she stripped from the neck down, rolled the dice and yelled, "Come on, baby, Mama needs new clothes!"

As the dice came to a stop she jumped up and down and squealed... YES! YES! I WON, I WON!"

She hugged each of the dealers and then picked up her winnings and her clothes and quickly departed.

The dealers stared at each other dumfounded.

Finally, one of them asked, "What did she roll?"

The other answered, "I don't know - I thought you were watching."

The Moral of the story is: Not all blondes are dumb, but all men are men.

****

There was an 80 year old virgin who suddenly got an itch in her crotch area!

She goes to see the doctor, who checks her over and tell her she has crabs.

She explained that she couldn't have crabs because she was a virgin and never shared her bed, but the doctor didn't believe her, so she went to get a second opinion.

The second doctor gave her the same answer, so she went to a third doctor and said "Please help me, This itch is killing me and I know I don't have crabs because I'm still a virgin and I have never shared my bed.

The doctor checks her over and says," I have good news and bad news."

The good news is you don't have crabs," the bad news is that your cherry has rotted and you have FRUIT FLIES.........

****

There were two golfers on the Golf Course

One of the men pulled out a cigarette and asked His friend for a light.

His friend pulls out a 12 inch Bic lighter. "Wow where did you get that large Bic"?

"Oh my Genie got it for me"

"Your Genie? You have a Genie? Where is he?"

"He is in my Golf Bag"

The friend says, "Can I see him?"

"Yes sure".

So the friend looks in the bag and out comes the Genie.

The man says to the Genie "I am your master's best friend, will you grant me one wish?"

The Genie says, "Yes just one wish"

So the man wishes for a million bucks.

The Genie goes back into the bag without saying a word.
Pretty soon the sky starts to get dark, and then it gets even darker.

The man looks up and sees a million ducks flying overhead.

"What's up with your Genie? Is he hard of hearing? I said a million bucks not a million ducks"

His friend says to him "Do you really think I asked for a 12 inch Bic

****

In case you needed further proof that the human race is doomed through stupidity, here are some actual label instructions on consumer goods.

On Sears hairdryer:

"Do not use while sleeping." - (Gee, that's the only time I have to work on my hair.)

On a bag of Fritos:
"You could be a winner! No purchase necessary. Details inside." - (The shoplifter special.)

On a bar of Dial soap:
Directions: Use like regular soap." - (And that would be how ...?)

On some Swanson frozen dinners:
"Serving suggestion: Defrost." - (But it's *just* a suggestion.)

On Tesco's Tiramisu dessert (printed on bottom of box):
"Do not turn upside down." - (Too late!)

On Marks & Spencer Bread Pudding:
"Product will be hot after heating." - (As night follows the day . . .)

On packaging for a Rowenta iron:
"Do not iron clothes on body." - (But wouldn't this save more time?)

On Boot's Children's Cough Medicine:
"Do not drive a car or operate machinery after taking this medication." - (We could do a lot to reduce the rate of construction accidents if we could just get those 5-year-olds with head-colds off those forklifts.)

On Nytol Sleep Aid:
"Warning: May cause drowsiness." - (One would hope.)

On most brands of Christmas lights:
"For indoor or outdoor use only." - (As opposed to what?)

On a Japanese food processor:
"Not to be used for the other use." - (I gotta admit, I'm curious.)

On Sainsbury's peanuts:
"Warning: contains nuts." - (Talk about a news flash.)

On an American Airlines packet of nuts:
"Instructions: Open packet, eat nuts." - (Step 3: Fly Delta.)

On a child's superman costume: - "Wearing of this garment does not enable you to fly." - (I don't blame the company. I blame parents for this one.)

On a Swedish chainsaw:
"Do not attempt to stop chain with your hands or genitals."
(Was there a spate of this happening somewhere? My God!)

****

It was Postman Pat's last day on the job after 35 years of carrying the mail through all kinds of weather to the same neighbourhood.

When he arrived at the first house on his route, he was greeted by the whole family there, who all hugged and congratulated him and sent him on his way with a gift cheque.

At the second house they presented him with fine Cuban cigars in an 18-carat gold box.

The folks at the third house handed him a case of 30-year old Scotch whisky.

At the fourth house a dumb blonde in her lingerie met him at the door. She took him by the arm and led him up the stairs to the bedroom where she blew his mind with the most passionate sex he had ever experienced.

When he had had enough they went downstairs, where the dumb blonde fixed him a giant breakfast: eggs, tomatoes, ham, sausage, blueberry waffles, and freshly squeezed orange juice. When he was truly satisfied she poured him a cup of steaming coffee. As she was pouring, he noticed a note sticking out from under the cup's bottom edge.

"All this was just too wonderful for words," he said, "but what's the five pound note for?"

"Well," said the dumb blonde, "last night, I told my husband that today would be your last day, and that we should do something special for you. I asked him what to give you".

He said, "Fuck him. Give him a fiver." She smiled prettily. "The breakfast was my idea."

****

Ethel is a bit of a demon in her wheelchair, and loves to charge around the nursing home, taking corners on one wheel and getting up to maximum speed on the long corridors.

Because she and her fellow residents are all one sandwich short of a picnic, they tolerate each other.

One day, Ethel was speeding up one corridor when a door opened and Mad Mike stepped out of his room with his arm outstretched. "STOP!" he said in a firm voice. "Have you got a licence for that thing?"

Ethel fished around in her handbag and pulled out a Kit Kat wrapper and held it up to him. "OK" he said, and away Ethel sped down the hall.

As she took the corner near the TV lounge on one wheel, Weird William popped out in front of her and shouted, "STOP! Have you got proof of insurance?"

Ethel dug into her handbag, pulled out a beer coaster and held it up to him. William said, "Carry on, ma'am."

As Ethel eared the final corridor before the front door, Bonkers Brian stepped out in front of her, stark naked, holding a very sizeable (for his age) erection in his hand.

"Oh, no!" said Ethel,

"Not the breathalyser again!"

****

Four men went golfing one day. Once on the course, three of them headed to the first tee and the fourth went into the clubhouse to take care of the bill. The three men started talking, bragging about their sons.

The first man told the others, "My son is a homebuilder and he is so successful that he gave a friend a new home for free. "

The second man said, "My son was a car salesman and now he owns a multi-line dealership. He's so successful that he gave a friend a new Mercedes, with all the extras.

"The third man, not wanting to be outdone, bragged, "My son is a stockbroker and he's doing so well that he gave his friend an entire stock portfolio.

"The fourth man joined them on the tee after a few minutes of taking care of business. The first man mentioned, "We are just talking about our sons. How is yours doing?

"The fourth man replied, "Well, my son is gay and dances in a gay bar." The three friends looked down at the grass and smirked.

The fourth man carried on, "Admittedly I'm not totally thrilled about the dancing job, but he must be doing pretty well. His last three boyfriends gave him a house, a brand new Mercedes, and a stock portfolio

****

A guy is nearing the end of his senior year in high school. Unfortunately, he still has to share a room with his younger brother who is only 9 years old.

One night, he decides to bring his girlfriend home for a little fun.

They have bunk beds and the guy notices that his little brother is already asleep on the lower bunk, so he and his girlfriend climb up to the top bunk.

As you might expect things start to heat up. The guy remembers that his little brother is sleeping below so he tells his girlfriend to whisper "lettuce" if she wants it harder and "tomato" if she wants a new position.

Lettuce!!!
Lettuce!!!
Lettuce!!!
Lettuce!!!

Lettuce!!!
Lettuce!!!
Tomato!!!

Lettuce!!!
Lettuce!!!
Lettuce!!!
Lettuce!!!
Lettuce!!!
Lettuce!!!
Tomato!!!

Lettuce!!!
Lettuce!!!
Lettuce!!!
Lettuce!!!
Lettuce!!!
Lettuce!!!
Tomato!!!

She screams.
Lettuce!!!
Tomato!!!
Whoa!!!
PULL IT OUT!!!
PULL IT OUT!!!

Then the little brother shouts up, "Hey, would you guys stop making sandwiches up there! You're getting mayonnaise all over my face!*!*!

****

David Beckham decides to try horseback riding, even though he has had no lessons or prior experience.

He mounts the horse unassisted and the horse immediately springs into motion.

It gallops along at a steady rhythmic pace as Victoria stands back in admiration, but then he begins to slip from the saddle.

In terror he grabs the horse's mane, but cannot seem to get a firm grip. He tries to throw his arms around the horse's neck, but he slides down the side of the horse anyway.

The horse gallops along, seemingly unaware of its slipping rider.

Finally, he gives up his frail grasp and he attempts to leap away from the horse and throw himself to safety.

Unfortunately, his foot has become entangled in the stirrup; he is now at the mercy of the horse's pounding hooves as his head is struck against the ground over and over again.

Posh stands there frantic, unable to do anything to help as his head is battered against the ground.

He is mere moments away from unconsciousness, perhaps death, when to his great fortune.....

The Supermarket security guard sees him, leans over, and unplugs the horse.

****

I was in the pub with my mates the other day, when a man came in and started drinking at the bar.

After a while, he pointed at me & shouted "I've shagged your mum!"

I decided it was best to ignore him and he resumed his drinking at the bar

Ten minutes later he comes back. "Your mum's sucked my cock!"

Again I ignored him - he then continued to drink, alone at the bar.

Ten minutes later he's back again and announces, "Oi! I've had your mum up the arse!"

By now I'd had enough, so I stood up & shouted up "Look dad, you're drunk, now piss off home!"

****

Two women are new arrivals at the pearly gates and are comparing stories on how they died.

1st woman: I froze to death.

2nd woman: How horrible!

1st woman: It wasn't so bad. After I quit shaking from the cold, I began to get warm and sleepy, and finally died a peaceful death. What about you?

2nd woman: I died of a massive heart attack. I suspected that my husband was cheating, so I came home early to catch him in the act. But instead, found him all by himself in the den watching TV

1st woman: So what happened?

2nd woman: I was so sure there was another woman there somewhere that I started running all over the house looking. I ran up into the attic and searched, and down into the basement.

Then I went through every closet and checked under all the beds. I kept this up until I had looked everywhere, and finally I became so exhausted that I just keeled over with a heart attack and died!

1st woman: Too bad you didn't look in the freezer. We'd both still be alive.

****

A fireman is polishing a fire engine outside the station when he notices a little girl next door in a little red wagon with little ladders hung off the side and a garden hose tightly coiled in the middle.

The little girl is wearing a fire fighter's helmet and has the wagon tied to a dog and cat. The fire fighter walks over to take a closer look.

"That sure is a nice fire truck," the fire fighter says with admiration.

"Thanks," The girl says.

The fire fighter looks a little closer and notices the girl has tied one wagon leash to the dog's collar and one to the cat's testicles.

"Little Partner," the fireman says, "I don't want to tell you how to run your fire engine, but if you were to tie that rope around the cat's collar, I think you could probably go a lot faster."

The little girl pauses for a moment to think, looks at the wagon, at the dog and at the cat, then shyly looks up into the fireman's eyes and says......

"You're probably right, but then I wouldn't have a f*#king siren, would I?!"

****

Eleven people were clinging precariously to a wildly swinging rope suspended from a crumbling outcropping on Mount Everest.

Ten were blonde, one was a brunette.

As a group they decided that one of the parties should let go. If that didn't happen the rope would break and everyone would perish. For an agonising few moments no one volunteered.

Finally the brunette gave a truly touching speech saying she would sacrifice herself to save the lives of the others.
The blondes all applauded.

Think about it

****

Big Australian guy's going down the road with a sheep under each arm.
Meets a mate who says "G'day mate. Ya shearing?"

"Nah", says the Aussie, "Gonna F*ck 'em both meself"

****

Several years ago, Great Britain funded a study to determine why the head of a man's penis is larger than the shaft. The study took two years and cost over $180,000. The results concluded that the reason the head of a man's penis is larger than the shaft is to provide the man with more pleasure during sex.
After the results were published, the French declared that the British were wrong and decided to conduct their own study of the same subject.

After three years of research and a cost in excess of $250,000, they concluded that the head of a man's penis is larger than the shaft to provide the woman with more sexual pleasure.

When the results of the French study were released, Australia decided to conduct its own study. So, after nearly three weeks of intensive research and a cost of around $75, the Aussies study was complete. They came to
The conclusion that the reason the head of a man's penis is larger than the shaft is to prevent his hand from flying off and hitting him in the forehead.

****

Kylie Minogue ,Robbie Williams & Will Young are out on the town on the piss.

Upon leaving Jongleurs nightclub, Kylie, somewhat the worse for wear, trips down the steps and lurches forward ramming her head between two railings.

Robbie seeing this wastes no time and lifts her skirt, slips her panties to one side and gives her a right royal seeing to.

After a few frantic minutes he is satisfied and turns to Will and says "come on mate it's your turn."

Will bursts into tears.

Robbie asks "Whats wrong? Come on, she wont remember a thing in the morning."

Will sobs inconsolably "I can't get my head between the railings"!!

****

A woman goes into a petshop, but isn't certain what sort of pet she wants. She looks at the cats...but no. She looks at the puppies...but no.

She is on the point of giving up, when she sees a beautiful Parrot at the back of the shop. She asks the shopkeeper how much it is and is told it is only £20.

She asks him why such a beautiful bird is only £20, and is told that it had come from a bad home, and its language can be extremely ripe.

Nevertheless, she decides to buy it. She gets the Parrot home and takes the cover off its cage. All the Parrot says is "Good afternoon, madam, new house, very nice." The woman is delighted, and wonders what the shopkeeper was talking about.

Later her two teenage daughters come home from school, and the Parrot says "New girls, very nice." Again the woman is delighted to have such a polite bird.

That evening, he husband, Dave, comes home from work. As soon as the Parrot sees him, it says "New brothel, new madam, new whores, but the same old customers...How are you Dave!"

****

2 SARS bugs leave the pub after a night of drinking.....one turns to the other and says, 'Bloody Hell, I could murder a Chinese'.

****

The other day I phoned my local pizza delivery firm and asked for a thin and crusty supreme they sent me Diana Ross.

****

There was a man who entered a local paper's pun contest. He sent in ten different puns, in the hope that at least one of the puns would win. Unfortunately, no pun in ten did.

****

A little girl goes to the barber shop with her father. She stands next to the barber chair, eating a cake while her dad gets his haircut. The barber smiles at her and says, "Sweetheart, you're gonna get hair on your muffin." "I know," she replies. "I'm gonna get tits too."

****

Scientist today exhumed Beethoven from his grave, when they opened the coffin; they were shocked to see him playing the piano backwards, when asked what this meant a spokesman said he was de-composing.

****

Sky has just won the rights to screen the first World Origam Championships from Tokyo. Unfortunately it's only available on Paper View......

****

Sean Connery gets a call from his agent one day. The agent goes "Sean,
I've got you a job, starts tomorrow, early. You'll have to be there for 10-ish".

Sean furrows his brow and says "Tennish but I don`t even have a racket."

****

A man gets shipwrecked on a desert island. His only companions in the boat are a pig and an alsation.

After a few weeks, he's been pretty successful - built himself a shack and doing OK for food. The only problem is that he's really starting to miss sex.

He looks at the options open to him and looks at the alsation and the pig.

"Got to be the pig", he thinks. So, he starts screwing this pig and all of a sudden, the alsation bites him on the arse.

Bloody hell, he thinks - this isn't on.

The next day, he tries again - alsation sinks his fangs into his arse again.
Man goes for walk on seashore, trying to think what he's going to do about this.

He comes across a young woman, looking in a bad way, lying on the beach. He carries her back to his shack and spends the next week or so looking after her and getting her back to health.

After a week, she finally comes around and says to him "I am just so grateful for what you've done - anything I can do for you, just name it".

"Hmmm, he thinks", looking at this beautiful young thing lying two feet from him.

"Well, there is something", he says somewhat nervously.

"Yes, name it - anything at all - I'm yours"

"OK, can you take this fucking dog for a walk?"

****

A missionary suddenly realized that the one thing he hadn't yet taught the natives he served was how to speak English, so he takes the chief for a walk in the jungle.

He points to a tree and says to the chief, "This is a tree." The chief looks at the tree and grunts, "Tree." The missionary is pleased with the response.

They walk a little farther and the missionary points to a rock and says, "This is a rock." Hearing this, the chief looks and grunts, "Rock."

The missionary is really getting enthusiastic about the results when he hears a rustling in the bushes.

As he peeks over the top, he sees a couple of the natives in the midst of heavy sexual activity. Flustered, the missionary quickly says to the chief, "Riding a bike." The chief looks at the preoccupied couple briefly, pulls out his blowgun and kills them.

The missionary goes ballistic and yells at the chief that he has spent years teaching the tribe how to be civilized and kind to each other. "How could you kill these people in cold blood that way?" he demands.

"My bike," the chief replied.

****

A penguin is driving through Arizona (as they do) on a hot summer's day when he notices his oil light is on.

He gets out of the car and, sure enough, it's leaking oil all over the road. The penguin drives around the corner to a service station and asks the mechanic to take a look at it.

The mechanic says he has a few others to look at first but if he comes back in an hour he can tell the penguin what is wrong with his car. The penguin agrees and goes for a walk.

He finds an ice cream shop and thinks a big bowl of vanilla ice cream will really hit the spot since he's a penguin and it's Arizona in the summer, after all. He sits down at the counter and starts in on his ice cream.

Of course he has no hands so it is rather messy. By the time he is done he has ice cream all over his flippers and his mouth-a total mess.

He walks back to the service station and says to the mechanic, "Did you find out what is wrong with my car?"

The mechanic replies, "It looks like you've blown a seal."

"No no," says the penguin. "It's just ice cream!"

****

Jim and Mary were both patients in a Mental Hospital. One day while they were walking past the hospital swimming pool, Jim suddenly jumped into the deep end. He sank to the bottom and stayed there.

Mary promptly jumped in to save him. She swam to the bottom and pulled Jim out.

When the medical director became aware of Mary`s heroic act he immediately ordered her to be discharged from the hospital as he now considered her to be mentally stable.

When he went to tell Mary the news he said, `Mary, I have good news and bad news. The good news is you`re being discharged because since you were able to jump in and save the life of another patient, I think you`ve regained your senses.

The bad news is Jim, the patient you saved, hung himself with his bathrobe belt in the bathroom. I am so sorry, but he`s dead."

Mary replied, "He didn`t hang himself, I put him there to dry"

****

There's this old priest who got sick of all the people in his parish who kept confessing to adultery. One Sunday, in the pulpit, he said, "If I hear one more person confess to adultery, I'll quit!"

Well, everyone liked him, so they came up with a code word. Someone who had committed adultery would say they had "fallen."

This seemed to satisfy the old priest and things went well, until the priest died at a ripe old age. About a week after the new priest arrived, he visited the mayor of the town and seemed very concerned.

The priest said, "You have to do something about the sidewalks in town. When people come into the confessional, they keep talking about having fallen."

The mayor started to laugh, realizing that no one had told the new priest about the code word.

Before the mayor could explain, the priest shook an accusing finger at the mayor and said, "I don't know what you're laughing about, your wife fell three times this week."

****

The Nun teaching Sunday school was speaking to her class one Sunday morning and she asked the question, "When you die and go to heaven, which part of your body goes first?"

Suzie raised her hand first and said "I think it's your hands".

"Why do you think it's your hands?" asked the Nun

Suzie replied...."because when you pray, you hold your hands together in front of you, and so God takes your hands first."

"What A wonderful answer!" The Nun replied.

Then Little Jonny raised his hand and said; "I think it's your legs"

"Oh and why is that Johnny?" The Nun asked

Little Jonny replied, "well last night I walked in to my Mum and Dad's room and mum was on the bed with her legs up in the air shouting "Fuck me, Oh God I'm coming!" if Daddy hadn't pinned her down we'd have lost her forever!"

****

A beautiful woman loved growing tomatoes, but couldn't seem to get her tomatoes to turn red.

One day whilst walking she came across a gentleman neighbour who had the most beautiful garden full of huge red tomatoes. She asked: "What do you do to get such red tomatoes?"

The gentleman responded: "Well, twice a day I stand in front of my tomato plants and expose myself - my tomatoes turn red from blushing so much!"

The woman was so impressed; she decided to try doing the same thing to her tomatoes to see if it would work. So twice a day for two weeks she exposed herself to her garden hoping for the best.

One day the gentleman was passing by and asked the woman: "By the way, how did you make out? Did your tomatoes turn red?"

"No" she replied, "but my cucumbers are enormous.........."

****

Big Fred came home after he'd been to the chemist with a pack of 100 scented condoms and said to his wife, "If I put a condom on, would you be able to tell me what scent it is?"

The Bride said, "No worries, should be able to guess that."

A few moments later, she said, "That one is CHEESE scented".

Fred said, "Hold it; I haven't put one on yet!!"

****

There's this newly-married couple who move into a house. The wife goes upstairs and notices a mirror hanging on the wall. She goes up to and says "Mirror mirror on the wall, what part of my body does my husband like most of all?" And the mirror replies "Your tits".

She then says "Mirror mirror on the wall, give me size 44!". And hey presto, she gets these big tits.

Excitedly she rushes downstairs to show her husband, who is amazed upon seeing her. He asks her what happened and she tells him about the mirror.

So the husband rushes upstairs to the mirror and says "Mirror mirror on the wall, what part of my body does my wife like most of all?" The mirror replies "Your dick". So the man says "Mirror mirror on the wall, make my dick touch the floor".

So his legs fall off...

****

Prince Charles finds an ancient wine bottle in the cellar of Windsor Castle. When he opens it a genie flys out and grants him a wish.

Charles is ecstatic as just that morning he had reversed his Range Rover over the Queen's favourite corgi and squashed it flat. He asks the genie to bring back the dog to life as the Queen would be furious and upset.

The genie examines the dog which is splattered all over the drive and tells Charles that there is nothing he can do so he'd best chuck the dog in the dustbin.

Charles then asks the genie if he could make his wife Cammilla beautiful as the media were always poking shit at her looks.

The genie thinks for a moment scratches his head and says "On second thoughts get that fucking dog out of the bin again"!!!

****

Two strangers were seated next to each other on the plane when the first guy turned to a beautiful blond and made his move by saying, "Let's talk. I've heard that flights will go quicker if you strike up a conversation with your fellow passenger."

The blonde, who had just opened her book, closed it slowly, and said to the first guy, "What would you like to discuss?"

"Oh, I don't know," said the player. "How about nuclear power?"

"OK," said the blond. "That could be an interesting topic. But let me ask you a question first.

"A horse, a cow, and a deer all eat grass. The same stuff. Yet a deer excretes little pellets, while a cow turns out a flat patty, and a horse produces clumps of dried grass. Why do you suppose that is?"

"Oh brother," said the guy. "I have no idea."

"Well, then," said the blond, "How is it that you feel qualified to discuss nuclear power when you don't know shit?"

****

A couple was celebrating their golden wedding anniversary. Their domestic tranquility had long been the talk of the town - "What a peaceful and loving couple."

A local newspaper reporter was inquiring as to the secret of their long and happy marriage. "Well, it dates back to our honeymoon," explained the man. "We visited the Grand Canyon and took a trip down to the bottom of the canyon by pack of mule.

We hadnt gone too far when my wifes mule stumbled. "My wife quietly said, that's once.

"We proceeded a little further and the mule stumbled again. Once more my wife quietly said, 'That's twice.'

"We hadnt gone a half-mile when the mule stumbled the third time.
"My wife quietly removed a revolver from her purse and shot the mule dead.

"I started an angry protest over her treatment of the mule, when she looked at me and quietly said, "That's once"

"And we've lived happily ever after."

****

Everybody who has a dog calls him "Rover" or "Rex." I call mine Sex.

Now Sex has been very embarrassing to me.

When I went to renew his dog license, I told the clerk I would like to have a license for Sex.

He said, "I would like to have one, too."

Then I said, "But this is a dog!"

He said he didn't care what she looked like.

Then I said, "But you don't understand. Ive had Sex since I was nine years old."

He said I must have been quite a kid.

When I got married and went on my honeymoon, I took the dog with me. I told the hotel clerk that I wanted a room for my wife and me and a special room for Sex.

He said every room in the place was for sex.

I said, "You don't understand. Sex keeps me awake at night!"

The clerk said, "Me too."

One day I entered Sex in a contest, but before the competition began, the dog ran away.

Another contestant asked me why I was just standing there looking around. I told him I had planned to have Sex in the contest.

He told me I should have sold my own tickets.

"But you don't understand," I said, "I had hoped to have Sex on TV."
He called me a show-off.

When my wife and I separated, we went to court to fight custody of the dog.

I said, "Your honour, I had Sex before I was married." The judge said, "Me too."

Then I told him that after I was married, Sex left me. He said, "Me too."

Last night Sex ran off again. I spent hours looking around town for him.

A cop came over to me and asked, "What are you doing in this alley at 4:00 in the morning?"

I said, "I'm looking for Sex."

My case comes up Friday

****

Three convicts were on the way to prison. They were each allowed to take one item with them to help them occupy their time whilst stuck behind bars.

On the bus, one turned to another and said, "So, what did you bring?"

The second convict pulled out a box of paints and stated that he intended to paint anything he could. He wanted to become the "Grandma Moses of Jail".

Then he asked the first, "What did you bring?"

The first convict pulled out a deck of cards and grinned and said, "I brought cards. I can play poker, solitaire and gin, and any number of games."

The third convict was sitting quietly aside grinning to himself.

The other two took notice and asked, "Why are you so smug? What did you bring?"

The guy pulled out a box of tampons and smiled. "I brought these."

The other two were puzzled and asked - "What can you do with those?"

He grinned and pointed to the box and said, "Well according to the box, I can go horseback riding, swimming, roller-skating..."

****

An old farmer is having trouble getting his bull to breed with the cows and is lamenting the fact to a few of his friends down the local beerhall.

One of them says, "You know Ben, I used to have the same trouble with my bull, but I got it fixed really quick".

"How did you get it fixed?"

"Well I just dipped my finger in the cow's vagina and rubbed it all over the bull's nose and he got right up her".

Ben goes home to the farm and decides to try it.

He grabs a cow, dips his fingers in the cow's vagina and rubs it all around the bull's nose.

The bull get's a rip roaring boner and immediately get's it right up the cow.

Ben was impressed.

That night, Ben gets into bed with his wife and can't get the effect on the bull out of his mind.

As she lays sleeping, Ben dips his fingers into his wife's vagina and feeling that it's nice and wet, he rubs it all around his nose and get's a rip roaring hard on.

He quickly shakes his wife awake and cries out, "Honey look!"

She rolls over, turns on the light and says, "You mean you woke me up in the middle of the night just to show me that you have a nosebleed?"

****

This bloke with Tourette's syndrome walks into the most exclusive restaurant in town.

"Where's the pissing, motherfucking manager, you cocksucking arsewipe?" he inquires of one of the waiters. The waiter is taken-aback and replies,'Excuse me sir but could you please refrain from using that sort of language in here. I will get the manager as soon as I can'.

The manager comes over and the bloke asks, 'Are you the chicken-fucking manager of this bastard place? 'Yes sir, I am,' replies the manager, 'but I would prefer it if you could refrain from speaking such profanities in this, a private restaurant'.

'Fuck off' replies the bloke 'and where's the fucking piano? 'Pardon?' says the manager. 'Fucking deaf as well, are we? You snivelling little piece of shit, show me your cunting piano.

'Ah,' replies the manager, 'you've come about the pianist job' and shows the bloke to the piano. 'Can you play any blues? 'Of course I fucking can,'

The bloke proceeds to play the most inspiring and beautiful sounding honky-tonk blues that the manager has ever heard. 'That's superb. What's it called? 'I tried to shag yer missus on the sofa but the springs kept hurting my dick,' replies the bloke.

The manager is a bit disturbed and asks if the bloke knows any jazz. The bloke proceeds, playing the most melancholy jazz solo the manager has ever heard. 'Magnificent,' cries the manager. 'What's it called? 'I wanted a wank over the washing machine but I got my balls caught in the soap drawer'.

The manager is a tad embarrassed and asks if he knows any romantic ballads. The bloke then plays the most heartbreaking melody the manager has ever heard, 'And what's this called?' asks the manager. As I fuck you under the stars with the moonlight shining off your hairy ring-piece,' replies the bloke

The manager is highly upset by the bloke's language but offers him the job on condition that he doesn't introduce any of his songs or talk to any of the customers.

This arrangement works well for a couple of months until one night, sitting opposite him, is the most gorgeous blonde he has ever laid his eyes on. She's wearing an almost see through dress, her breasts are almost falling out the top of her black lace bra, and the skimpy little 'G string she's wearing is doing very little to conceal her ample charms.

She's sitting there with her legs slightly open, sucking suggestively on asparagus shoots as the butter is dripping down her chin. The image is too much for the bloke and he scurries off to the Gents to furiously masturbate.

He's tugging away furiously when he hears the manager's voice. 'Where's that bastard pianist? He just has time to relieve himself, and in a fluster he runs back to the piano having not bothered to adjust himself properly, sits down and starts playing some more tunes.

The blonde steps up and walks over to the piano, leans over and whispers in his ear, 'Do you know your knob and bollocks are hanging out your trousers and dripping spunk on your shoes? The bloke replies 'Know it? I fucking wrote it.

****

A hippie gets onto a bus and sits next to a nun in the front seat. The hippie looks over and asks the nun if she would have sex with him. The nun, surprised by the question, politely declines and gets off the bus at the next stop.

When the bus starts on its way, the driver says to the hippie, "For a fiver, I can tell you how you can get that nun, to have sex with you".

The hippie says that he'd love to know, & hands over the fiver! So the bus driver tells him, that every Tuesday evening at midnight, the nun goes to the cemetery and prays's to God. "If you went dressed in a robe and glow in the dark paint mask, she would think you are god and you could command her to have sex with you".

The hippie decides this is a great idea, so on Tuesday he goes to the cemetery and waits for the nun to show up.

At midnight, sure enough the nun showed up, while she was in the middle of praying, the hippie jumped out from hiding and says. "I AM GOD" I have heard your prayers and I will answer them BUT ... first you must have sex with me.

The nun agrees, but asks for anal sex so she might keep her virginity because she is married to the church. The hippie eagerly agrees to this and has his way with the nun.

After the hippie finishes, he stands up and rips off the mask and shouts "Ha, Ha Ha guess what, I'm the hippie!!"

Then the nun jumps up and shouts "Ha Ha Ha guess what, I'm the bus driver!!"

****

In a classroom of third graders, the teacher says to the kids, "Today, class, we will be telling stories that have a moral to them." She explained what a moral to a story was and asked for volunteers. Little Suzie raises her hand.

Suzie: "I live on a farm and we have a chicken that laid 12 eggs, we were excited to have 12 more chickens but only 6 of them hatched."

Teacher: "That's a good story, now what is the moral?"

Suzie: "Don't count your chickens before they are hatched."

Teacher: "Very good Suzie, anyone else?"

Ralphie: "Yes teacher, I was carrying some eggs I bought for my mom in my bicycle basket one day and I crashed my bike and all the eggs broke."

Teacher: "That's a nice story, what is the moral?"

Ralphie: "Don't put all your eggs in one basket."

Teacher: "Very good Ralphie, anyone else?"

Little Johnny: "Yes teacher, my Aunt Karen is in the army and when she was in the Gulf War, she parachuted down with only a gun, 20 bullets, a knife, and a six-pack of beer. On her way down, she drank the six pack. When she landed, she shot 20 Iraqis and killed ten of them with her knife."

Teacher: "Very interesting, Johnny, what is the moral to your story?"

Little Johnny: "Don't fuck with my Aunt Karen when she's drunk."

****

Wife looks in the mirror and says "Look at me, I am fat, wrinkly and ugly"

She turns to her husband and says "Pay me a compliment"

Husband replys "your eyesight is great".

****

Three Ducks Walk Into a Pub,

The Barman Says To The First Duck, Whats Your Name Little Duck. The Duck Replies, My Names Huey and I've Been In and Out Of Puddles All Day Lo

That's Nice It Seems As Though Youve Had a Nice Day.

The Barman Turns To the Second Duck, And Whats Your Name Little Ducky.

My Names Duey and I've Been In And Out Of Puddles All Day and I've Really Enjoyed It.

The Barman Turnes To The Third Duck And Says, I Suppose Your Name Is Louie Little Duck.

The Duck Replies, No My Names Puddles and Dont Ask Me What Sort Of Day I've Had

****

I phoned my boss told him I couldnt make it in today as I was sick

Boss: "how sick are you we`re really busy here today?"
Me: "I`m fuckng my sister"

****

Three dead bodies turn up at the mortuary, all with very big smiles on their faces.

The coroner calls the police to tell them his results after the examination.

"First body: Frenchman, 60, died of heart failure while making love to his girlfriend. Hence the enormous smile, Inspector," says the Coroner.

"Second body: "Scotsman, 25, won a thousand pounds on the lottery, spent it all on whisky. Died of alcohol poisoning, hence the smile."

The Inspector asked, "What of the third body?" "Ah," says the coroner," this ... is the most unusual one. Paddy from Belfast, 30, struck
By lightning."

"Why is he smiling then?" inquires the Inspector.
"Thought he was having his picture taken."

****

An Australian, an Irishman and a Scouser were sitting in a bar. There was only one other person in the bar. The three men kept looking at this other man, for he seemed terribly familiar.

They stared and stared, wondering where they had seen him before when suddenly the Irishman cried out "My God! I know who that man is - it's Jesus!" The others looked again, and sure enough, it was Jesus himself, sitting alone at a table.

The Irishman calls out across the lounge "Hey! Hey you! Are you Jesus?" Jesus looks over at him, smiles a small smile and nods his head. "Yes, I am Jesus," he says. Well, the Irishman calls the bartender over and says to him: "I'd like you to give Jesus over there a pint of Guinness from me." The bartender pours Jesus a Guinness. Jesus looks over, raises his glass in thanks and drinks

Then the Australian calls out "Oi you! D'ya reckon you're Jesus or what?" Jesus nods and says "Yes, I am Jesus". The Australian is mighty impressed and has the bartender send over a pot of Fosters for Jesus which Jesus accepts with pleasure.

The Scouser then calls out "Oi wack, would you be Jesus?" Jesus smiles and says "Yes, I am Jesus". The Scouser beckons the bartender and tells him to send over a pint of bitter for Jesus, which the bartender duly does. As before, Jesus accepts the drink and smiles over at the table.

Finally, after finishing the drinks, Jesus leaves his seat and approaches our three friends. He reaches for the hand of the Irishman and shakes it, thanking him for the Guinness. When he lets go, the Irishman gives a cry of amazement: "Oh God! The arthritis is gone! The arthritis I've had for years is gone! It's a miracle!!!"

Jesus then shakes the Australian's hand, thanking him for the lager. Upon letting go, the Australian's eyes widen in shock. "By jingo mate, the migraine! The migraine I've had for 40 years is completely gone it's a miracle!!!"

Jesus then goes to approach the Scouser who says: "Back off mate - I'm on Disability...

****

Printed in Great Britain
by Amazon